MANIPUR ON FIRE

EYEWITNESS TO ETHNIC STRIFE AND SURVIVAL

RAJAN CHAUDHARY

Made with ♥ on the Notion Press Platform
www.notionpress.com

Contents

Author's Note

In the summer of 2023, the northeastern state of Manipur became the epicenter of one of the most devastating ethnic conflicts in recent Indian history. The violence that erupted in May scarred communities, displaced thousands, and left behind stories of loss, resilience, and survival that demand to be heard.

As a journalist with The Mooknayak, I stood at the crossroads of history, documenting the voices of those too often silenced by mainstream narratives. This book is not just a recounting of events but an attempt to bring to light the faces behind the headlines—the mothers, the children, the elders, and the countless others whose lives were upturned.

In August 2023, with limited resources and budget, I chose to travel by train from Lucknow to Dimapur, Nagaland—the nearest accessible point to Manipur. From there, the only route into Manipur lay through the mountains, where local wingers (a type of shared bus) are the lifeline for those commuting.

The journey from Dimapur to Imphal was grueling and risky. Slippery roads winding through the mountains led to repeated bouts of sickness. I vomited several times during the ride, all while navigating illegal extortion by unidentified groups along the way. Armed men interrogated us at multiple points, making the trip harrowing for a first-timer like me.

The reports covered in this book revolve around human rights violations and the harsh realities that unfolded after the ethnic clashes between the Kuki-Zo and Meitei communities in June 2023. Violence raged as I wrote these stories—Manipur remained cut off from the world with internet shutdowns, and bloodshed divided its people.

Completing this project meant trekking kilometers on foot, gathering facts from highly sensitive regions, and crossing buffer zones at my own risk. Every step was taken without backup or assurance of safety.

"Manipur on Fire" is a testament to the resilience of those who survive in silence and those who continue to fight for justice. Each page echoes the footsteps I followed through relief camps, villages, and smoldering streets of Manipur.

— Rajan Chaudhary, Journalist

Jan 2025

Preface

The story of Manipur is not just one of conflict and suffering but also of resilience, courage, and the unyielding human spirit. As the northeastern state became engulfed in ethnic violence during the summer of 2023, the lives of countless individuals were irrevocably altered. This book, "Manipur on Fire: Eyewitness to Ethnic Strife and Survival," seeks to bring forth the voices that are often drowned out by the cacophony of political narratives and media coverage.

The journey to document these stories began with a simple yet profound commitment—to uncover the truth and illuminate the realities faced by the people of Manipur. In a time when the state was shrouded in fear and uncertainty, Rajan Chaudhary, a journalist with The Mooknayak, embarked on a perilous path to stand witness to history as it unfolded. His travels took him across the rugged terrains of the northeastern hills, through volatile checkpoints, and into the heart of communities torn apart by violence.

What emerged from these travels is not just a chronicle of the events that transpired but a testament to the enduring spirit of those who refuse to be silenced. From the mothers in relief camps struggling to care for their newborns to the young children yearning to return to school amidst burnt books and shattered homes, each account reveals a fragment of the larger mosaic of Manipur's struggle.

This book does not claim to offer all the answers. Instead, it seeks to ask the right questions. Why did the conflict escalate to such devastating levels? What role did historical grievances, political decisions, and socio-economic conditions play? And most importantly, how can the road to peace and reconciliation be paved for future generations?

As readers delve into these pages, they will encounter stories of heartbreak but also of hope—of communities finding ways to rebuild, of individuals standing in solidarity, and of the unwavering belief that justice and peace are not beyond reach.

It is our hope that "Manipur on Fire" will serve as both a historical record and a call to action, urging policymakers, civil society, and ordinary citizens to engage deeply with the complexities of ethnic strife and work collectively toward a more inclusive and harmonious society.

Rajan Chaudhary's courage and dedication remind us all of the power of journalism to bear witness, to give voice to the voiceless, and to inspire change. May this book stand as a beacon, shedding light on the path forward for Manipur and for all those who believe in the transformative power of truth.

—Rajan Chaudhary

Acknowledgements

I owe this book to the unwavering support of my colleague Satya Prakash Bharti, who stood by me throughout this journey. These stories were originally penned in Hindi, and I am grateful to Geetha Sunil Pillai for translating them into English, ensuring they reach a global audience. I am also deeply thankful to my mentors at The Mooknayak—Managing Editor Arun Kumar Verma and Editor-in-Chief Meena Kotwal—whose guidance and encouragement made this possible.

CHAPTER ONE

Imphal - A Meitei-dominated city nestled in a beautiful valley

Amid the shadows of tension and disruption, life in Manipur's Imphal is slowly inching back to its usual rhythm, although traces of unease persist. I journeyed to the heart of the matter, beyond the surface numbers and statistics, to truly understand the impact of the ongoing discord.

In the heart of Manipur is its capital Imphal, a city teeming with cultural diversity and history, where a recent eruption of violence has cast a shadow over the lives of its residents. Nearly three months have elapsed since the clash between the Kuki and Maitei communities ignited, setting off a cauldron of discord that reverberated throughout Manipur.

Yet, as one strolls through the bustling streets of the state capital, an air of semblance seems to have returned. Essential shops adorn the streets and the lively Imphal market radiates a renewed spirit. Despite this, a nighttime curfew remains, a precautionary measure for security reasons.

Setting out with resolve, I embarked on a mission deep into the core of the issue. My intention was resolute: to transcend the boundaries of mere numbers and analytical reports.

My journey led me to ground zero, where I aimed to uncover the human stories concealed beneath the surface, stories that often defy quantification in statistical terms.

Khaidam Subsas, a forty-two-year-old denizen of Moyrong Thong, a residential enclave within Imphal, embarked on constructing his dream abode a few days prior to the outbreak of violence. The conflict had inadvertently disrupted the flow of construction materials, leaving Subsas and many others grappling with scarcity.

Subasas tells me, "The fear has subsided a bit now. It is a little fine here (Imphal city) but our people who are in the mountains have a lot of problems in front of them. The situation was very bad 2-3 months ago. When we started building houses, all this happened. There is no construction material in the shops here, due to which the workers have also returned to their homes due to the closure of work. The workers are finding it difficult to find because they have to return home early. There is a curfew here in the evening," he says. "The children are going to school hardly once or twice a week, being given leave by the schools for other days."

Notably, the curtain of curfew was drawn across Manipur in the aftermath of the violence, necessitating the deployment of over forty thousand security personnel, including soldiers and paramilitary forces. The twilight hours are governed by curfew, from 6 p.m. to 5 a.m., during which only medical facilities are operational. Attendance at school has become sporadic, a mere once or twice a week, as schools accommodate the reality of life under curfew.

Tiken Sharma, a sixty-year-old proprietor of a neighborhood shop, shares the palpable aftermath of the violence on his business. Formerly bustling with customers from near and far, the shop now witnesses only a trickle of footfall.

"Right now, the prices of everyday commodities like pulses, sugar, milk, potatoes, tomatoes etc. have increased. Because since the incident in the hill, things coming from outside have been limited. In the early days of violence, people were not allowed to come out of their houses at all. Those who had the goods available at that time sold them at double or thrice the actual price and made profits," Tiken Sharma told me. The supply chain disruptions have led to shortages and price hikes, leaving vendors like Sharma struggling to navigate these challenging times.

Imo Sharma, a retired government teacher who used to instruct English and Social Studies to Class 10 students in a government school, now finds himself in a different landscape. With Class 12 classes underway, there is a notable absence of nursery schools having reopened. The anticipation, however, is that they will resume operations soon. This is because the presence of a significant number of army forces has necessitated the transformation of the school premises, where the children once studied.

"The disruption caused by the dispute has severed the supply lines of goods from outside the state. Consequently, the availability of everyday essentials has dwindled, affecting the accessibility of necessary items for the local populace," explains Imo Sharma to me. The government is currently reliant on private trucks and specialized transportation for the transportation of goods. These goods undergo stringent scrutiny at the state border, overseen by vigilant security forces.

In a promising development, Sharma reveals that government offices are gradually resuming their operations. People are slowly returning to their official routines and responsibilities, marking a step towards restoring a sense of normalcy in the midst of ongoing challenges.

I met Poitang, a 45-year-old man who supports his family by maneuvering an electric e-rickshaw in the bustling precincts of the Imphal market. Setting off from his home at 9 a.m. each day, he embarks on a quest to secure passengers. However, the tides have shifted.

In what were once ordinary times, Poitang would typically rake in a daily income of Rs 800 or even more. Yet, since the onset of the ethnic violence incident, the narrative has changed dramatically. The number of passengers has dwindled significantly, casting a pall over his earnings. Presently, his daily income hovers around Rs 300—a stark contrast to the financial security he once enjoyed.

Notably, the indomitable spirit of Manipur's women shines through as they take the reins of commerce. A remarkable phenomenon unfolds across the capital, with women steering vegetable stalls, clothing boutiques, roadside markets, and even domestic enterprises. From haggling over prices to overseeing both modest and grand establishments, these women exemplify resilience, courage, and a determination to secure not only their own livelihoods but also that of their families.

In the face of uncertainty, the intricate web of Manipur's society weaves a tale of resilience, adaptation, and the unwavering spirit that propels a community forward, even in the midst of adversity.

As a vegetarian, I often find it challenging to have my food arranged. Ronaldo, the worker at "Manipur House" hotel, faces similar difficulties when trying to accommodate my dietary preferences. On the other hand, my colleague Satya Prakash Bharti, who enjoys non-vegetarian food, has no such issues. I don't mind at all that he eats meat. One day, I bought two plates of chowmein from a shop in Imphal market. Just as I was about to eat, Satya Prakash stopped me, pointing out that there were pieces of finely chopped meat in the chowmein, which I had mistaken for soybean. The woman at the shop, seeing my concern, quickly washed her utensils and prepared a fresh plate of chowmein without meat for me.

In Manipur, non-vegetarian food is ubiquitous, with almost every fast-food shop and hotel serving it, even amidst the ongoing violence. Very few shops remain open in the city, yet the sale of meat, particularly from pigs and other large animals, is a common sight. It's interesting to note that, despite the Bharatiya Janata

Party's (BJP) claims of promoting purity and sattvic living, banning the sale and purchase of meat from larger animals in a state governed by the BJP alliance seems unlikely.

Our preparations to travel to Churachandpur, a Kuki-dominated area, had begun in earnest. We had already visited numerous relief camps in the Meitei-majority valley, but to truly understand the contours of the conflict tearing Manipur apart, it was imperative to witness the other side. I felt a personal pull towards Churachandpur, driven by curiosity and a sense of journalistic duty.

Our base was near Norem Thong in Imphal city, where the weight of the conflict was palpable. The violence that had engulfed the state was not a distant echo; it lived in every hushed conversation and in the wary eyes of the people. We had learned that entering the most sensitive zones and reporting from curfew-imposed areas required special identification issued by the State Information Commission. Without hesitation, I decided that the day would be dedicated to securing the necessary documents and preparing for the journey ahead.

Among our preparations, one item stood out – a black press jacket. It was not just a garment but a shield, a silent declaration of neutrality in a landscape polarized by fear and suspicion. With the internet blackout and language barriers, the jacket served as a visual cue, signaling that we were observers, not participants. The memory of a female journalist from "Aaj Tak" being allegedly assaulted at her hotel in Imphal lingered in our minds, reinforcing the urgency of this precaution.

By noon, our identification cards were issued, bearing the official insignia that granted us passage. With the paperwork in hand, we set out to find a tailor capable of crafting the press jackets. Our search led us to "KEN BAG Industries" in East Imphal, a professional establishment humming with the sound of sewing machines. As we waited for the jackets to be stitched, an elderly man seated nearby fixed his gaze upon us, his curiosity almost tangible.

"Who are you people, and where have you come from?" he inquired, his tone teetering between suspicion and intrigue.

I introduced myself and explained our purpose in Manipur. "We're heading to Churachandpur tomorrow. We need these jackets for the trip," I added casually, not anticipating the shift in his demeanor.

His eyes narrowed, and his voice dropped an octave. "Why do all the journalists want to go to Churachandpur?" he asked, a trace of bitterness seeping through his words. "Go ahead, go. The Kuki people have plenty of money. They grow opium and smuggle it across the border. You'll see it for yourself."

It was evident he was Meitei. His words dripped with the acrimony of a community entrenched in conflict. "They're dangerous," he warned, his voice laced with an unsettling certainty. "Barbaric people. They kill without mercy."

For a fleeting moment, his words unsettled me. The image he painted was vivid and grim. But the journalist in me sensed more than just caution in his voice; there was an undercurrent of intent, a desire to deter. Perhaps he hoped we would do as others had – skim the surface in Imphal and return with half the story.

But that was not an option. The road to Churachandpur beckoned, and so did the stories waiting to be told.

CHAPTER TWO

Why Only Muslim Drivers Can Enter Churachandpur?

"In times of war, the loudest truths are often whispered by those who suffer most."

— Anonymous

Manipur has become divided after the recent outbreak of violence. Neither Kukis nor Maiteis are venturing into each other's territories. However, there exists a single Muslim community that can navigate freely between these two groups, acting as a neutral bridge between them.

"Would you take us to Churachandpur?" In the city of Imphal, if you inquire about traveling to Churachandpur, you're likely to receive consistent advice from regular auto, rickshaw, and winger van drivers: "Who would risk their life going there amidst the ongoing firing?"

This sentiment is echoed unanimously by regular auto drivers, rickshaw operators, and winger van drivers. Moreover, a consistent piece of advice emerges from these conversations: if you're intent on heading to Churachandpur, it's best to have a Pangal Muslim driver at the helm.

The prevailing apprehension among these drivers reflects the volatile situation that has gripped Churachandpur. Their unanimous warning speaks volumes about the atmosphere of uncertainty and potential peril surrounding the area. And the suggestion to opt for a Pangal Muslim driver carries a sense of trust and security—a tacit acknowledgment that such drivers possess an unmatched familiarity with the terrain and the dynamics at play. Moreover, they are neutral, which means they have no hostility towards either of the warring communities, and hence, commuting with them is believed to be safe.

Arif, an Imphal resident who owns a Swift Dzire car, has undertaken numerous journeys to Churachandpur, the most volatile region in the state. He has even transported media personnel to the area.

To uncover the situation in Churachandpur, locals from Imphal and the hotel owner where I was staying recommended employing a Muslim driver for the journey. Arif, when approached, agreed to the task. He quoted a fare of Rs 8,000 for the perilous journey of approximately 63 km to the tense and violence-stricken hill area from the capital. Despite the offered assistance, I opted to venture on my own with the aid of local vehicles and security forces.

Starting from the capital city Imphal and heading to the Moyrong Khoyol Cathal Market, and subsequently to the PHOUGAKCHAO Police Station, any regular driver could only take you up to this point. Beyond this juncture, neither the driver's courage nor the security forces would permit further progress for a non-Kuki driver. Essentially, it's understood that only a Muslim or Kuki driver is allowed to proceed, as an unspoken agreement with the security forces.

The security forces have established numerous checkpoints preventing movement towards Churachandpur. These checkpoints, including some manned by Kuki individuals, halt vehicles and conduct inspections. They scrutinize the occupants, inquire about their identity, destination, and inspect their government ID cards and vehicle details. Only after satisfactory answers are provided, and the driver's entry is noted with a signature in the checkpoint's register, are vehicles allowed to continue. This protocol is frequently followed along the route.

Why are only Muslim drivers entrusted with travel to Churachandpur? Bashir, a 25-year-old resident of Imphal, explains, "We aren't involved in the conflict between Maitei and Christian (Kuki community), so we're granted safe passage in both directions." He further adds, "Our population is relatively small, and staying among Kukis would lead to our demise. If we reside with Maitei, Kukis might target us. Hence, we remain impartial."

A representative from Kangla Tours & Travels, a cab service in Imphal, reveals, "While we possess a fleet of vehicles, we exclusively deploy Muslim drivers for journeys to Churachandpur."

In contrast to the mainstream media's portrayal of negative sentiment against Muslims, and the reported instances of mistreatment in BJP-governed states, Manipur paints a different picture. Muslims serve as a vital link in transporting people between the two conflicted areas of Maitei and Kuki, who harbor mutual antipathy. Amidst this animosity, only Muslim drivers have facilitated movement and communication.

The tension between the Kuki and Maitei communities is so severe that even government employees avoid entering non-community-dominated territories. In the fraught atmosphere, the government employees avoid venturing into areas not aligned with their own community. This deep-seated division has created an environment of apprehension and avoidance among those tasked with maintaining civic functions. I faced challenges while trying to return from Churachandpur. I sought assistance from Churachandpur's Deputy Commissioner and security forces to traverse the region. However, even on the way out, Kuki individuals halted the official vehicle, questioning my identity. The government vehicle's Kuki driver informed them that he could only accompany me to Kangwai due to the risk of violence erupting on sight.

This animosity between the Kuki and Maitei communities has resulted in a complete avoidance of each other's areas. The sole exception is the Muslim drivers, who transcend this divide, facilitating safe passage for individuals with no affiliations to either community.

CHAPTER THREE

Women's Ordeal in Manipur's Relief Camps, Newborn Lives in Jeopardy

From the struggle to find a semblance of privacy for breastfeeding to the discomfort of changing sanitary pads frequently due to post-delivery bleeding, their experiences have been marked by hardship. Amidst the relentless days of adversity, these women have been denied the luxury of freely sharing their thoughts, forced to coexist in cramped relief camps with unfamiliar faces.

History bears witness to the painful reality that conflicts often cast men into clashes while women and children bear the harshest consequences. In the wake of three months of turmoil in Manipur, the plight of women, particularly expectant mothers and nursing women, in relief camps has been a tragic tale. Both Meitei and Kuki women have borne the heaviest burdens. From the struggle to find a semblance of privacy for breastfeeding to the discomfort of changing sanitary pads frequently due to post-delivery bleeding, their experiences have been marked by hardship.

Amidst the relentless days of adversity, these women have been denied the luxury of freely sharing their thoughts, forced to coexist in cramped relief camps with unfamiliar faces.

Nearly three months after the violence in India's northeastern state of Manipur, the hilly Meitei community and the Valley-based

Kuki community are forced to abandon their broken, burnt-out homes and save their lives in relief camps in community-dominated areas. It has increased that the Maitei who used to live in the hills have moved to the Maitei-dominated areas or relief camps in the valley after the violence, while the people of the Kuki community who used to live with Maitei earlier have now moved to Kuki-dominated areas or hilly areas.

Churachandpur district, located in a tribal-dominated hilly region 63 km from the capital Imphal, is home to the largest number of people belonging to the Kuki tribe. Although many tribes are living here, the narrative of describing other tribes settled in the hills as Kuki can also be seen throughout Manipur since the violent clash between the majority Maitei and the minority Kuki that began on May 3rd.

Zerry, 35, a volunteer at a relief camp set up by the YVA (Young Vaiphei Association) in an old school building near IB Road District Hospital Churachandpur, shared that around 100 relief camps have been set up in the district. Zerry, who works at Select City Mall in Delhi, had come to his home in March this year after which the violence took place. Then he could not return to work again.

Lamvah Touthang, 33, who lives in the relief camp, gave birth to a baby girl on May 31st, the next day after she arrived at the relief camp. Somehow, she managed to save her life with her husband. Through the forests, she reached this relief camp a month later.

When Lamvah and her husband ran away from home, they had neither money nor clothes. They had nothing but the only clothes they were wearing.

"Every morning, my husband leaves the relief camp in search of work to arrange for milk to feed the child, diapers to wear, medicines. But there is no work in such a situation."

"The violence started near Utangpokpi village in Chandel district. People were being shot and their houses were being burnt. Seeing this, we also left our house to save our lives and reached here through the forest. The baby was born at the Churachandpur district hospital the next day after coming to the camp. We didn't have a single piece of clothes when we ran away from home. After the daughter was born, we did not even have clothes to dress her. She is now 2 months old; she needs warm water to be bathed, clothes to wear, and medicines. But there is no money. My husband has had no work since the violence began."

"My BP (blood pressure) goes down while sitting here thinking about what to feed, what to wear, what the future will be. I checked the doctor several times. After having a baby, the mother needs protein-rich food, but I have nothing. We have no remedy for these mental sufferings. We demand from the central government that we get separate administration so that we can get peace, we can return to our normal life," said Lamvah Touthang in a frustrated tone.

Lamvah alleges that the central government is providing facilities, medicines, food to the people of the Maitei community living in Maitei relief camps, but the relief camps of the Kuki community are being ignored. "The Maitei people are getting food and other necessities from the central government in relief camps. There, things are being distributed daily to the people by the government. But nothing is found here. There is a shortage of milk, medicines, and food grains for the child; we demand from the central government and the state government that we should also be given medicines and food."

Lhingkhotin, 25, who is six months pregnant, arrived at the relief camp on May 17th from Utangpokpi village with two of her family members and her 3-year-old son.

As a pregnant mother, when asked about the availability of diet and medicines in the relief camp, Lhingkhotin said, "There is nothing but dal and rice in the food here. Money is needed to buy other things that are not available. What is available in the camp here, we have to eat this food to survive."

She adds, "Sometimes paracetamol, vitamin medicines are available from the relief camp when there is a fever, but the relief camp does not have enough money to give us enough medicines. The road between Imphal and Churachandpur are blocked. Nothing is coming from outside. Whatever little is being received here, is coming from Mizoram. The things that are available here are also expensive. Things for a balanced diet are available from the market, but you need money to buy! Who will give us? ...We have no choice. should we die of bullet or of hunger!"

"The media is saying it was ethnic violence, but we believe it was state-sponsored violence on tribal people," Lhingkhotin shared in her local dialect. "Our houses were burnt, we ran into the forest to save our lives, then escaped to the relief camp."

Christy, aged 30 and hailing from the YVA relief camp, sheds light on the pivotal support offered by the church, contributing 90 percent of funds to sustain camp operations. Expressing concern, Christy laments the absence of government assistance, questioning the sustainability of their current situation.

Turning to another relief camp in Churachandpur district, we delve into the Rengkai Relief Camp housed within a converted high school complex. This haven accommodates 378 IDPs (Internally Displaced Persons), encompassing 191 male victims and 187 female victims. Among them, 72 families have sought refuge from the violence, alongside 99 boys aged 17 and above, and 87 individuals within various relief camps. Furthermore, the camp shelters 30 boys and 27 girls aged above 5 years, reflecting the varied demographics of those seeking solace.

Fleeing the confines of Sugunu village in Churachandpur district following a dispute in May, Boithem, 23, and her husband Lalminthang, 30, left their home immediately after facing an attack. Lalminthang, Boithem's husband, shared their ordeal regarding medical support following the birth of their child. "After the childbirth, the district hospital provided some medication. Yet, subsequently, we were informed of the unavailability of necessary medicines," he conveyed, expressing his remorse for being unable to provide his wife with the vital nutritious sustenance she requires as a new mother.

Voicing her apprehension over nurturing her child in the confines of the relief camp, Boithem divulged her heartache, revealing, "When the echoes of sobbing reverberate in this room, my child's cries resonate even more. Yet, our hands are tied – we have no alternatives. The future remains uncertain, veiled in ambiguity."

In an attempt to grasp the government's stance on the ordeal within the relief camps grappling with the scarcity of medicines and ration deficits in Churachandpur district, we sought an audience with Deputy Commissioner (DC) Dharun Kumar and asked about the inadequacy of medical provisions for the health-related concerns faced by the displaced inhabitants.

He said in such a situation people may be facing various health issues, although the government is making best efforts to provide food supplies in these camps. Moreover, Churachandpur DC offered insights into the comprehensive list outlining relief camp names and the corresponding materials slated for distribution, unveiling the administration's approach to address these pressing concerns.

CHAPTER FOUR

Condition of Women and Newborns at Maitei Relief Camp

Nestled 45 kilometers from the capital Imphal, the Khoyol Keithel Camp in the Moirang area shelters a total of 269 IDPs (Internally Displaced Persons), predominantly hailing from the Maitei community. Among them, 36 children and 32 girls, aged between 1 and 12, have sought refuge since the outbreak of ethnic violence.

Tamphasana Loima, a 24-year-old, fled her home when the conflict between the Kuki and Maitei communities ignited. Taking refuge in a makeshift camp in Moirang, she arrived on May 3 with her five-month-old child. With a voice laden with tears, she confided, "Both my child and I are unwell. The community members managing this camp are offering support. We were attacked by the Kuki people, compelling us to seek safety here." Her voice quivering, she continued, "Every day since my arrival, I've shed tears. I long to escape this situation, to reunite my family and regain a sense of normalcy through work."

Residing in the relief camp alongside her husband and other family members, Tamphasana has spent months grappling with insecurities, health challenges, and familial distress. She shared, "The Kuki people razed our homes to the ground. Where can we possibly find shelter now? They're inflicting harm and occupying our spaces. The turmoil they ignited continues unabated. Why subject innocent lives to such havoc? Fear has gripped all of us here, a fear that defies articulation. We're trapped in an indescribable existence."

Assisting the distressed as a volunteer at the Khoyol Keithel Camp, Kumam, aged 35, shared that the majority of those seeking refuge at the relief camp belong to the Maitei community.

Among them is Sumila's (24) entire family, who have resided in the same relief camp since May 3. Six months pregnant, Sumila navigates her circumstances alongside her first child, one-year-old Denson. While governmental hospitals offer complimentary check-ups and medicines, some prescriptions remain unfulfilled, necessitating purchases from external medical sources. The financial constraint poses challenges in securing the required medications, although the compassionate individuals within the relief camp provide monetary assistance for this purpose.

Crucially, the relief camp's location is over 45 kilometers away from Imphal. This geographical reality accentuates concerns, particularly for pregnant women who must navigate such distances in precarious circumstances. The specter of violence looms, rendering these journeys even more unsettling. This worry is further compounded by the presence of Kuki people in several areas of Imphal, where the Maitei community resides amidst potential unrest.

Sumila clarified that her house remained unscathed by the flames, yet her family fled the premises driven by fear upon witnessing the violence unfold in close proximity.

Laisham Priya, 29, who lives in a relief camp located just 5 kilometers from Imphal, spoke with us about the profound psychological toll exacted by the turmoil. She shared, "The violence has forced us to seek refuge. The future remains uncertain, and the prevailing atmosphere is thick with uncertainty. Families are suffering immensely."

Laisham Priya, with her seven-month-old baby girl, said, "There is a lack of everything. We need more support and attention from the government. There is no money, no work."

Sanatombi Chanu, 23, a first-year BA student, also lives in the relief camp with her family. "Our house was burned. We had to flee, leaving everything behind. Now, we are scattered in different relief camps, unable to see each other's suffering," she said.

Regarding the health concerns of pregnant women, Chanu said, "There is no provision for the delivery of pregnant women here. The limited food supply will directly affect their health and the health of their babies."

In a heartening display of resilience, the Konjengbam Community Hall organized training for women to create makeup products, giving them a chance to generate income and become financially independent. However, the trainer, Rimson Wangjam, clarified that for now, the training is limited to the Maitei camps due to safety concerns.

K. Anand Singh, the administrator of the Konjengbam Community Hall, shared the initial struggles the camp faced and the vital support from local businesses and social organizations. Despite financial constraints, the camp has continued to provide food and shelter to those affected by the violence, though Anand Singh has called on the government for a timely resolution.

A makeshift facility for bathing and changing has been set up using plastic sacks, though it falls short in providing privacy and safety for the women living in the camp.

The camp's water source is a pond that is not ideal for drinking or washing due to contamination. Women in the camp are forced to draw water from this pond, posing significant hygiene challenges.

The roots of the ethnic violence that has plagued Manipur are multifaceted, involving political, territorial, and social factors. The Meitei community's demand for Scheduled Tribe (ST) status, along with the Kuki community's concerns over their rights, government actions on drug cultivation, and a rumor that sparked the conflict, have all contributed to the violence.

CHAPTER FIVE

Unveiling the 'Outsider' Narrative and Revealing the Lives of Hill Dwellers

Churachandpur, a tribal-dominated hilly district, has become the focal point of intense discussions and sensitivities following ethnic violence. The division of Churachandpur in Manipur into two parts after the violence has led to growing suspicion. The investigation reveals a crucial fact: not all tribal communities in Churachandpur are outsiders; indeed, many tribal families have been residing here since before India's independence.

In May, after an incident of ethnic violence in the eastern Indian state of Manipur, the Maitei community in the Valley openly asserted that the Kuki community in the hills were outsiders, suggesting they should be sent back to their supposed home country. However, as I ventured into Churachandpur district, predominantly inhabited by the Kuki community, I uncovered layers of inconsistencies and falsehoods in these claims.

As I traveled along the main road of Muolvaiphei Village, the stones lining its hillsides stood as silent witnesses to the rich history embedded within this community. While my original purpose was to locate an unfamiliar relief camp, my attention was captivated by three particular stones positioned at the roadside. I stopped and embarked on a curious investigation.

Within the village of Muolvaiphei, there are presently over 800 households, with a total population exceeding 2,300 residents. Predominantly Christian, they are members of the tribal community. The village primarily comprises Mizos and Hmar tribes, deeply rooted in their Mizo and Hmar heritage. Lalzarlien Darngawn, aged 83, serves as the village's second leader, following in the footsteps of his father, the village's initial head.

Lalzarlien shared a captivating piece of history: In 1911, when his father first arrived here, there were merely one or two dwellings on this hill. "My father played an instrumental role in establishing this village. The cultivation of paddy began here under his guidance, and since then, we have called this place our home," remarked Lalzarlien Darngawn to me.

Prior to arriving in Churachandpur, I had conducted inspections of relief camps situated in several areas of Manipur predominantly inhabited by the Maitei community. These visits had revealed simmering resentment among the Maitei people towards the Kuki community. Some had even labelled the Kuki residents as outsiders, suggesting they hailed from Verma, Myanmar. Seeking clarity on this matter, I posed the question to Lalzarlien Darngawn, asking him, "To what extent is it true that you are referred to as outsiders?" His response was unequivocal, as he politely asserted, "Completely untrue."

Lalzarlien seemed somewhat disheartened by my inquiry. However, before delving further, he cordially invited me to sit down, expressing his desire to share something significant. After a brief wait, he emerged from a room in his house, clutching a large-page album diary and a collection of documents. In that moment, it became apparent that he was about to reveal something he had held onto for years, a piece of history he had chosen not to share until now.

Our amazement grew as we turned the initial pages of the album's diary. Within its pages lay a photograph captured by none other than the former Prime Minister, Morarji Desai. Lalzarlien could be seen presenting a shawl in that picture. Subsequently,

Lalzarlien embarked on a journey through his personal history, revealing one significant moment after another through the album's pages. The extraordinary nature of these historical snapshots was evident. One particular photo in the album dated back to 1978 when Lalzarlien attended a presentation in the Tribal Chief Delegation on Republic Day.

Furthermore, Lalzarlien shared a document that held great significance. It was the record of Muolvaiphei attaining the status of a village, as published in the *Manipur Gazette* by the Government of Manipur on August 16, 1956. This listing placed Muolvaiphei as the 131st village in the Gazette, demonstrating that the village had met all the government criteria for village status in 1956, despite having already been settled there for some time.

However, despite this evidence, incidents of violence in the state have not dissuaded some Maitei individuals from continuing to describe all hill tribal residents as illegal migrants. Lalzarlien Darngawn also provided me with a copy of the order he received, instructing the transfer of the chiefship of Muolvaiphei Village to him on January 11, 2013, issued by Lacintha Lazarus, the deputy commissioner of Churachandpur.

Raghu Singh, a 66-year-old retired IRB resident of Khoyol Keithal Camp in the Maitei community located in the Moirang area, approximately 45 km from the capital Imphal, expressed his perspective to me, stating, "The Kuki people have come from Myanmar. No Kuki is Manipuri. They are fighting for possession of the land. You guys should appeal to the honorable Prime Minister to remove them." Raghu Singh holds the belief that all Kukis have originated from outside the region.

It's essential to note that the violence in this region has led to hundreds of casualties on both the Kuki and Maitei sides, with thousands displaced from their homes. Consequently, there is a prevailing sentiment on both sides that the other has committed wrongdoings.

Speaking anonymously, the woman chairperson of a social organization in Churachandpur district emphasized the historical roots of Muolvaiphei village, asserting that it was settled long before the country's independence. She pointed out that the government has not adequately developed this area, despite its longstanding presence, and that institutions and colleges have primarily been established in Imphal, leaving the village with limited resources.

It's crucial to recognize that not all Kukis can be labeled as outsiders. Solicitor General Tushar Mehta, representing both the Central and Manipur governments, addressed the violence in the state before the Supreme Court in August. During a half-day-long hearing on the Manipur violence, he stated, "Most of the unclaimed bodies killed during the violence belong to infiltrators." Following this statement, there was a surge of media coverage, leading to a narrative being disseminated across the country, including in the state, that Churachandpur's tribals are outsiders. However, families like Laljarlin Darngawn's challenge this perception, as they have their roots in Mizoram and have been settled here long before India's independence.

Following Solicitor General Tushar Mehta's statement, a rumor began to circulate that all residents of Churachandpur district in the hills were Kukis, which is far from the truth. The ground report reveals that a substantial number of tribal communities reside here, but not all tribals belong to the Kuki community. Over the years, Hindu, Bengali, Muslim families, and numerous families from Bihar have also established their homes in Churachandpur district. However, the heavy presence of security forces guarding the borders of the district, especially during the violence between the Kukis and Maitei, has created geographical and ideological divisions among its people.

In response to these divisions, many in the region advocate for a separate administration as a potential solution to the ongoing issues. The tribal communities here are calling for a 'separate administration' from the Manipur government.

S. Dongthin Sang, aged 30, challenges the portrayal of hilly tribes as 'illegal immigrants' in media reports by citing his family's long-standing presence in the region. He points to his maternal grandmother's age and the birth of the state's Chief Minister to emphasize the depth of their roots in the area. He disputes the 'illegal immigrant' label, noting that his grandmother Kopchin (105), was born in 1917, long before the Chief Minister came into the world.

He passionately asserts, "We are Indian citizens. My ancestors were Indian freedom fighters. Many of my family members serve in the Indian Army. We are not illegal immigrants. Prime Minister Modi ji, you are a great leader, and we appreciate you, but you have overlooked this critical issue." He further mentions that after a recent incident of caste violence in the state, Manipur Chief Minister N. Biren Singh pledged to find a political solution to the conflict and continue efforts to identify and address illegal immigration issues in the state.

CHAPTER SIX

Children Yearning to Return Home & School Amidst Burnt Books, Uniforms

A stark disparity emerges in this educational landscape – while children from the Meitei community living in proximity to their relief camps have been promptly admitted to nearby primary schools, their counterparts residing in the Kuki-dominated hill areas face an agonizing educational standstill. An anonymous employee from a social organization operating in Churachandpur district attributes this discrepancy to the ambivalence displayed by the Manipur government towards the Kuki community.

Three months after ethnic violence erupted in Manipur in May, the children who once attended school, college, and tuition are now confined to relief camps, their memories of education fading amid harsh conditions of insecurity, hunger, unemployment, and uncertainty.

An old boys' hostel near the IB Road District Hospital in Churachandpur district has been transformed into a makeshift relief camp by the Young Vaiphei Association (YVA). This hostel, situated in a tribal-dominated hilly area about 63 km from the capital Imphal, has seen better days. Despite its dilapidated condition, it now serves as a refuge, offering shelter from dust, thunderstorms, and rain to the displaced individuals.

On the second floor of this converted hostel, a group of girls huddles together in a corner. The presence of the team in the vicinity kindles a glimmer of hope in their hearts. For the first time in a long while, someone seems interested in addressing their concerns. As the team engages in discussions with some refugee tribal women in nearby rooms, their attention turns to these girls. Eager to share their experiences and hardships, these girls speak of their interrupted education and uncertain future.

These young girls, like so many others in similar situations, have been forced to put their education on hold. They have endured the trauma of fleeing their homes in the wake of violence, leaving behind not just their houses but also their school bags, books, and uniforms, all of which were lost to the flames of destruction.

One girl, a 13-year-old Class 7 student, tearfully recounted her ordeal. The violence erupted just as her exams were approaching, forcing her to abandon her education. Her family fled Utangpokpi village to save their lives, enduring a month in the forests. "Our houses were burned down. School bags, books, uniforms were burnt," she lamented, her fervent desire echoing through her tears: "I want to go back to my school again."

Sitting alongside her were Nengheikim, aged 16, and Chinneikim, aged 19, both Class 10 students. Their expressions conveyed the trauma they had endured. Words seemed inadequate to convey the depth of their experiences.

This crisis extends beyond these individual stories. The government has failed to provide a local education solution for these displaced children who were once attending school before the violence. With their houses razed to the ground, they face a daunting road ahead.

At the Rengkai Relief Camp in the Kuki-dominated Churachandpur district, 99 boys and 87 girls over the age of 17 grapple with the anguish of interrupted education. The YVA, in their commendable efforts, has set up over 100 relief camps across the district to aid those affected by the violence. Zerry, one of the volunteers, informed me. This staggering number underscores the sheer magnitude of tribal children who have been deprived of their education for months.

In this dire landscape, the story of Kailash, a 38-year-old resident running a small tea shop in Muolvaiphei Village in the tribal-dominated hills, brings into focus the harsh realities faced by these families. His two children, a daughter and a son, have been unable to attend school since May. His account reveals the difficulties they encounter in the aftermath of the violence, from skyrocketing prices of goods due to disrupted roads to their dire living conditions.

Kailash reveals, "The children had just completed one round of examinations when the school doors were abruptly closed. We've arranged for some tutoring to keep their studies alive." He also highlights the challenges of increased expenses due to the disruption of normal road access, making basic goods more costly. Kailash passionately expresses his concern over the ethnic violence and pleads for unity, emphasizing the need for government intervention.

The ethnic violence has inflicted a heavy toll on both the Kuki-zo minority tribal community and the Meitei majority community, causing not only social but also economic, educational, and ecological losses. Hundreds from both communities are stranded in relief camps. Yet, there's a stark contrast in the response; while Meitei children in the Valley have managed to secure local school admissions, the government has yet to extend a helping hand to Kuki children in the hills.

Imo Sharma, a retired government teacher living in the residential area of Naorem Thong, Imphal, shares his insights. He used to teach English and Social Studies to Class 10 students before the violence erupted. Regarding the education of affected children, he notes that while classes for Class 11 and 12 have recently resumed, nursery schools are yet to reopen. The presence of a significant number of army forces in the schools where these children used to study has contributed to this delay.

In the Moirang area, situated 45 km from the capital Imphal, the Khoyol Keithel Camp shelters a total of 269 IDPs (Internally Displaced Persons), predominantly from the Meitei community. Among them, 36 boys and 32 girls, aged between 1 and 12 years, have sought refuge in the camp since the outbreak of caste violence. Kumam Davidson, a dedicated relief camp volunteer at the age of 35, takes it upon himself to educate the youngest members of the camp, tirelessly teaching them within a room, assisted by fellow volunteers.

Laishram, another compassionate volunteer at the same relief camp, shared insights with me, revealing that nearly all the children from the relief camp attend a nearby school where they have secured free admission. The routine of these resilient children begins with school at 8 in the morning, concluding as they return to the relief camp by 3 in the afternoon.

A stark disparity emerges in this educational landscape – while children from the Meitei community living in proximity to their relief camps have been promptly admitted to nearby primary schools, their counterparts residing in the Kuki-dominated hill areas face an agonizing educational standstill. An anonymous employee from a social organization operating in Churachandpur district attributes this discrepancy to the ambivalence displayed by the Manipur government towards the Kuki community.

Speaking under the veil of anonymity, the female chairperson of the social organization lamented, "Before the country's independence, many villages were settled here in tribal-dominated Churachandpur. The government, however, neglected this area, labelling it as inhabited by illegal immigrants. While all the reputable colleges and institutions were established in Imphal, we were left with nothing here."

Max, a 28-year-old resident of the Konjengbam Relief Camp, once pursued his passion as a football player. Hailing from the Meitei community, Max attained education up to the 10th standard. His life took a tragic turn when his house in Churachandpur district was set ablaze by Kuki mobs during the violence. When questioned about his prospects of returning home, Max sighed, "What's the use of going back there? My home no longer stands, and I lack the means to rebuild it."

He continued to share the extent of his despair, "My entire life has been upended. In this tense atmosphere, there's no place to focus on my football preparations. My football club in Guwahati disbanded after a video, the infamous parade of naked women, went viral. Even my tickets were cancelled simply because I belong to the Meitei community. With no internet for over three months, I can't find work, and I'm left without any money in hand. We've been living like this for months," Max concluded, his tone reflecting the desolation marking the end of his career.

The impact of the ongoing violence is evident in Manipur's educational landscape, with security forces now occupying more than half of the state's schools and colleges. Following the outbreak of caste violence, a significant deployment of security personnel in the state has reshaped the educational environment. These security forces have found their bases within the students' institutions, leaving the young learners with no alternatives for their studies. The suspension of internet services in the state for over three months has compounded their challenges.

In the aftermath of the May violence, approximately 125 companies representing various paramilitary forces, along with around 164 companies from the Indian Army and Assam Rifles, have been stationed in conflict zones and tension-laden areas across Manipur. Each company comprises roughly 120-135 employees, and army contingents number between 55-70 soldiers. This formidable security presence has left Manipur's students with limited options for their education, as their schools and colleges have been transformed into security bases amid a tumultuous period.

CHAPTER SEVEN

Heartfelt Moment as Kuki Cancer Patient Asks, 'Can I Shake Hands?'

IDPs (Internally Displaced Persons) in the Kuki-dominated regions of Manipur are suffering from ailments like cancer, liver disease, and chickenpox while living in relief camps. Financial constraints prevent them from seeking treatment at private hospitals, and the aftermath of violence has left them unemployed. Allegedly, there is only one government hospital in Churachandpur to serve a population of over three lakh, facing a critical shortage of essential medicines. The growing tension between the Kuki and Meitei communities further complicates access to healthcare in the valley.

Lily, a tribal woman who sought refuge in the relief camp just two weeks ago, was diagnosed with a severe liver condition by doctors at the district hospital. Her frail and emaciated form speaks volumes of her suffering. Confined to a room shared with more than 30 fellow residents, her condition has left a lasting impact on everyone in the camp.

Rengkai, located in the tribal-dominated Churachandpur district, has become one of the most densely populated areas. The Rengkai Relief Camp, housed in a high school campus, accommodates 378 displaced people—191 men and 187 women—representing 72 families who fled various locations due to the violence. Lily is one of them.

Visiting the room where 45-year-old Lily resides, surrounded by women and children, was heartbreaking. It was difficult to watch her struggle to consume the rice and lentils provided at the camp. Despite encouragement from nearby residents to eat more, Lily's deteriorating physical condition left her unable to sit up unaided. The people in the camp are determined not to lose Lily, having already endured the loss of loved ones and homes. The women visit her throughout the day, offering help whenever needed.

Lily, from B-Gangte village, is a mother of four. However, in the camp, only her 12-year-old son, Lunjalin, is by her side, looking after her as she battles severe illness. Lunjalin's peers play around the camp, but he remains constantly by his mother's side. His meager earnings from the relief camp, supplemented by contributions from nearby residents, barely cover the costs of Lily's medication.

While struggling to sit for extended periods, Lily shared that one of her sons had passed away, and the whereabouts of her other two sons remain unknown since the violence erupted. She explained, "My married daughter sends money for medication, helping us keep the treatment going. When the pain becomes unbearable, the people here take us to the doctor." She could not say more about her plight.

Anthony, a volunteer at the Rengkai Relief Camp, provided insight into Lily's condition. He shared, "When we took Lily to Churachandpur District Hospital, we learned she has a severe liver problem. Unfortunately, we can't afford proper treatment, and the doctor told us they're out of essential medications. The suffering of people in this camp always brings tears to our eyes. What else can we do?" Anthony, with a kind heart, offered food to the team, saying, "You've come to my place, and I don't know if you've eaten or not. I've prepared some food for the camp; please have some. It's all I can offer." His gesture deeply touched us.

The story of another Kuki tribal woman at the Rengkai Relief Camp, Chinkhoneng Baite, 46, is even more distressing. She is battling breast cancer and spends most of her days sitting outside the relief camp's houses, trying to avoid burdening others with the sight of her illness.

Upon arriving at the Rengkai Relief Camp, other IDPs mentioned another cancer patient, and we set out to find Chinkhoneng. We found her sitting with her husband, Jamkhothang Baite (50), flipping through medical reports and prescriptions.

Chinkhoneng explained that her village, with over 100 houses, was set ablaze by Meiteis during the violence. Fearing for her life, she fled to an army camp, leaving behind her children— a son (7) and two daughters (11 and 8). After a week, her children were sent to her married daughter, and she eventually made her way to the Rengkai Relief Camp. Due to her incurable disease and the lack of resources, she and her husband have remained at the camp since.

Chinkhoneng, with tears in her eyes, expressed, "The treatment has been ongoing for 3-4 years, and I was diagnosed with cancer last year. Life has become incredibly hard. I worry about my daughters. Who will care for them? All of this drives me to despair."

Jamkhothang Baite, once a renowned professional football player, turned to farming after an unfortunate incident in 2011. However, after the violence, he faces unemployment. Before the conflict, he would graze goats in the hills.

"We sold our goats to a company, and all the money I earned from football went toward my wife's medication. The district hospital claims they don't have the necessary medicines. We are not receiving any government medical aid either. We are just barely getting by," Jamkhothang revealed.

He also shared the story behind his decision to quit football: "I had a Meitei friend who became jealous of my rising football career. He started giving money to Naxalite groups who threatened me to quit football, or I would be harmed. After 2011, I stopped playing." Anthony, the volunteer, corroborated Jamkhothang's story, describing him as the best football player of his era.

Chinkhoneng's cancer is incurable, and she lacks the means to receive timely dialysis. Her life is precariously hanging in the balance. Our visit to the tribal-dominated Churachandpur region was fraught with risk due to the tense atmosphere. As we prepared to leave, Chinkhoneng quietly asked, "Can I shake hands with you?" She wished to express her gratitude for drawing attention to the tribals' suffering. We obliged, and she exclaimed, "God Bless You!" Her heartfelt gesture left a deep impression on us, and we left without looking back.

In the Saikawt ITI relief camp, nestled in the Churachandpur district hills, three-and-a-half-year-old Seth is suffering from chickenpox. His family is struggling, unable to access the necessary medicines. His mother, Maryjona, 34, cares for him, while his father, Philip, 39, struggles to find daily wage labor in the difficult post-violence environment.

Philip is powerless due to financial constraints, preventing him from seeking treatment for Seth's condition. The district hospital doctors have reported that government medicines are unavailable. In the dead of night, Maryjona shows Seth's chickenpox-infested body with the light of a torch.

Maryjona said, "We have no choice but to quietly endure here. We have no money and no work. Our house was looted and set on fire. People identifying as Meiteis have come to the relief camp to save their lives."

Churachandpur district, with a population of 330,100, is served by just one government hospital. This disparity between the underdeveloped hills and the more developed valley raises serious concerns. The tense atmosphere in the hills has hampered transportation, affecting the supply of essential goods, medicines, and fuel. Prices in the hills have surged, leaving IDPs in the relief camps struggling, especially those with severe illnesses.

I met with Churachandpur Deputy Commissioner (DC) Dharun Kumar to inquire about the medicine shortage in the relief camps and the state government's plans to assist IDPs. When asked about the medicine shortage and healthcare challenges, the DC responded, "There is a medicine shortage across the country, and people are facing various health issues. Some medicines may not have been available. We still have some remaining medicines." The DC did not elaborate further.

Initially, the DC's response seemed somewhat dismissive of the IDPs' hardships.

However, my investigation uncovered deeply distressing conditions. The IDPs are not living; they are merely enduring each passing day. They have become refugees in their own land.

Furthermore, the IDPs in Churachandpur cannot easily access good hospitals in the valley for treatment.

Manipur has been divided following the caste violence that erupted in May. The valley is predominantly inhabited by the Meitei community, while the hills are home to the Kuki-Zo community. Both communities are segregated, with heavily guarded borders separating them. The buffer zone, through which essential supplies, including medicines, must pass, is frequently the site of gunfire, making transportation extremely difficult. As a result, people in the hills must make do with whatever resources they have.

There is also a severe shortage of medicines for HIV patients. Churachandpur reports a total of 4,239 HIV-positive cases, with 105 new cases detected between April and July 2022. Of these, 2,072 individuals are receiving ART treatment. Manipur accounts for 1.04% of India's HIV cases, representing 0.24% of the state's total population. Following the violence, a significant shortage of general and high-risk disease medications has emerged. Churachandpur Antiretroviral Center last received medicines from the Manipur State AIDS Control Society on June 24. The center's consultant revealed in August that no supplies had arrived since then due to the officer-in-charge, who was Meitei, fleeing to Imphal in May.

The consultant explained, "We are out of stock for Lopinavir 40 mg and Ritonavir 10 mg tablets required for children. We have no stock left, so we're breaking adult tablets in half to give them to children."

It is evident that the only government hospital in the Kuki-dominated area is facing a critical shortage of life-saving medicines. Without immediate intervention from the state or central government, hundreds of lives are at risk.

CHAPTER EIGHT

Concealing 'Churachandpur'

Churachandpur district, originally named after the Meitei king, Meidingngu Churachand (1886–1941), has seen a significant transformation in recent months. Government records reflect this name change to Churachandpur in honor of the Meitei king. However, after the outbreak of violence, the Kuki-Zo community has actively removed this name from various locations, especially in the Lamka area.

The situation in Manipur has become more distressing with the violence that erupted in May this year, leaving a deep divide between the Meitei tribes in the valley and the Kuki tribals in the hilly regions. The violence has created a situation where no community dares to venture into areas dominated by the other. The conflict has severely disrupted transportation across the region, further isolating communities and halting the flow of goods.

Churachandpur, situated in the hilly region of Manipur, is predominantly inhabited by the Kuki community. With a population exceeding three lakh, this district lies to the southwest of the capital, Imphal. In the aftermath of the violence, all road routes to Churachandpur have been heavily guarded by security forces, making it nearly impossible for vehicles or individuals to enter the area. After maintaining this status quo for months, the people of Churachandpur are now facing dire shortages of essential goods, including food grains, medicines, petrol, and diesel.

Pastor Khupdokhen, 57, a resident of New Lamka Gckveng in Churachandpur district, pointed out that vehicles traveling from Imphal to Churachandpur have been halted for months. Goods that are available are being sold at exorbitant prices. He said, "Petrol is being sold here for Rs 120 per liter because petrol supplies from Imphal have stopped. The petrol being sold by roadside vendors has been brought from Mizoram, hundreds of kilometers away," pointing to the petrol stored in cans by the roadside.

Numerous checkpoints have been set up by security forces at the borders of Churachandpur district. The areas connecting Churachandpur to other regions have been designated as buffer zones, with strict prohibitions on the entry of both Kuki and Meitei individuals. No Meitei can enter Churachandpur, and any attempt to do so could lead to violence. Similarly, no Kuki-Zo individuals are allowed to leave Churachandpur, as they are at risk in the valley areas where the Meitei population predominates. The security forces and local authorities emphasize the need to avoid encounters between the two communities to prevent further conflict.

Lianpu, 68, a retired BSF soldier and resident of Churachandpur district, advocates for a separate administration for the people of this district. He believes that the situation will improve if the district has its own governance. Lianpu stated, "Nothing is allowed to come from Imphal. Work has come to a standstill since the onset of the fighting. Even oil (petrol-diesel) is unavailable. It is brought in from Mizoram, 400 km away." He strongly emphasized, "Only when we have our separate administration can we survive. The Manipuri people tell us that they will drive us away from here."

Neng Boi, 37, a Kuki woman who runs a shop in New Lamka market, mentioned the skyrocketing prices of daily essentials. "The price of tomatoes in the market is Rs 250 per kg. After the violence, we are out of work, and people are staying indoors. We don't know how long this will continue," she said, reflecting the distress of the community.

The situation in the relief camps is equally concerning. Many Internally Displaced Persons (IDPs) in Churachandpur district are suffering from serious diseases and a severe shortage of medicines. Those who fled from violence-stricken areas and reached the camps are without jobs or financial support. Additionally, the district's only government hospital, which serves a population of over three lakh, has faced significant challenges in obtaining essential medications, leaving the community vulnerable to further health crises.

The ongoing violence has led to a profound shift in the cultural and political landscape of Churachandpur. The residents, who are primarily Kuki, have grown disillusioned with the Manipur government. As a response to the violence and their eroding trust in the administration, the people of Churachandpur have begun to erase or obscure the name 'Churachandpur' from public view. In its place, many areas now display inscriptions such as 'Kuki Land' or 'Tribal.' This act signifies a reclamation of identity and autonomy, reflecting the deep divide between the two communities.

David, a member of the Indigenous Tribal Leaders Forum (ITLF) in Churachandpur, has been at the forefront of advocating for the rights of the tribal community. He explained that Churachandpur was initially named after the Meitei king, Meidingngu Churachand, but following the outbreak of violence, the Kuki community has systematically removed this name from public spaces, particularly in Lamka.

With supply lines within the district largely closed off, the Kuki community has turned to Mizoram, located 400 kilometers away, as a primary source for essential goods. However, the journey to Mizoram is not without its challenges, and the distance only adds to the already soaring prices of commodities.

David emphasized that this change in name and identity is part of a larger struggle for autonomy. The community's quest for a separate administration is seen as the only way to protect their rights and ensure their survival. As the situation in Churachandpur continues to evolve, the people of Kuki Land remain resolute in their demands for justice, equality, and self-determination.

CHAPTER NINE

One Night in Churachandpur

My experience of spending one night in Churachandpur stands out as one of the most harrowing and unforgettable events of my life. The journey into this hilly terrain, marked by the constant challenge of passing through numerous security checkpoints, paled in comparison to the ordeal of returning from Churachandpur to Imphal. Traveling via Vishnupur, we eventually reached the buffer zone — an area strictly off-limits to the general public, under the heavy watch of Indian security forces. The absence of civilian vehicles on the main road heightened the tension.

For about an hour, we sat alongside the security personnel, hoping a passing vehicle would offer us a ride to Churachandpur. Eventually, a Bolero emerged from Imphal, carrying a young girl. The security forces halted the vehicle and requested the driver to take us along. After thorough scrutiny of our identities and purpose at multiple checkpoints, we were allowed to proceed.

During the journey, I conversed with the girl seated in the front. She held a few books, mentioning that she was preparing for an exam, but refrained from discussing the pressing unrest engulfing the region. Upon reaching Churachandpur, the driver dropped us outside the District Hospital, leaving us to navigate an unfamiliar town.

Our next objective was to locate nearby relief camps. However, language barriers and identity issues compounded our difficulties.

Mobile connectivity offered little help in identifying our location or guiding us further. The stares from passersby were unnerving, but our press jackets silently conveyed our mission. After persistent effort, we found a relief camp.

The camp sheltered numerous women and children, displaced by violence, living there for months. A volunteer advised us to contact the Indigenous Tribal Leaders' Forum (ITLF) for further assistance. The ITLF, a key advocate for the Kuki tribal community, actively liaised with the government to address tribal grievances and lead their movement.

Following this advice, we reached the ITLF office, where a member provided addresses of additional relief camps. His willingness to personally guide us to several camps was invaluable, given our unfamiliarity with the area. Over the course of the day, we visited three camps, gathering crucial information and documenting the plight of the displaced.

As night approached, we checked into Hotel Venus in New Lamka. The prevailing rumors of a potential attack by Meitei groups made sleep elusive. The air was thick with fear and uncertainty.

The next morning, we ventured into the local market of New Lamka, where women sold vegetables, aquatic plants, and live crabs bound to bamboo sticks — a sight that vividly illustrated the cultural distinctiveness of this northeastern state. Capturing these moments with our cameras inadvertently drew unwanted attention. A local woman, visibly agitated, confronted us, speaking loudly in her native tongue. Soon, a crowd encircled us.

Unable to understand her, I introduced myself in English. An elderly man intervened, recognizing our press affiliation. "We thought you were spies," he remarked, easing the tension. Our subsequent conversation revealed deep-seated distrust toward the Manipur government. In a tone heavy with frustration, he implored, "Convey our message to Modiji. We seek separate administration. If ignored, we may turn to China for help."

Returning from Churachandpur the next day— By afternoon, we returned to the ITLF office, visiting more relief camps and hill villages. As dusk approached, the thought of returning to Imphal loomed large. Outside the District Commissioner (DC) office in Churachandpur, we paused at the "Wall of Remembrance," a temporary memorial adorned with photographs of those lost to the violence. Kuki organizations had organized an event there.

Inside the DC office, District Commissioner Dharun Kumar briefed us on government initiatives aimed at restoring peace. Acknowledging the volatile situation, he arranged for an official vehicle to transport us to the Churachandpur border, the farthest point deemed safe for travel.

The driver, a Kuki man, voiced his apprehension. "I can't drive beyond this point. If Meitei groups see me, they won't spare me, even in a government vehicle," he confided. His words underscored the deep-rooted divisions plaguing the region.

Left at the border, we continued on foot to a security checkpoint. There, we met an army soldier from Pratapgarh, Uttar Pradesh. His friendly demeanor was a brief respite, but he too was bound by duty and could not accompany us further.

Undeterred, we pressed on, trekking nearly two kilometers through the buffer zone. Every step was fraught with peril, knowing that armed groups lurked unseen. Reaching another security checkpoint, we noticed "Kuki Land" scrawled across the barricades.

Finally, an auto-rickshaw driven by a Muslim man offered us passage into the Meitei-dominated valley. By evening, we arrived safely in Imphal, our hearts heavy with the memories of the people and the land we had left behind.

Even today, the memory of Churachandpur evokes a profound sense of unease. The rift between the Kuki and Meitei communities has widened, fueled by misinformation and entrenched grievances. Armed groups, unaffiliated with official security forces, roam freely, posing an ever-present threat.

As I reflect on the beauty of Manipur, I am left questioning the necessity of such violence in a land so rich in culture and history. The scars of conflict run deep, and the path to reconciliation seems fraught with obstacles. Yet, the resilience of the people endures — a testament to their hope for a better tomorrow.

CHAPTER TEN

Misinformation Fuels Manipur's Crisis

The violence-stricken state of Manipur has been rife with the circulation of fake news, even as authorities attempted to curb its spread by restricting internet access. The conflict between the majority Meitei community and the minority Kuki tribes recently garnered global attention after a horrific video of two women being assaulted and paraded naked by a mob went viral, sparking outrage in India and abroad.

However, alongside these tragic events, false claims about sexual violence and other incidents further fueled the state's volatile situation. Women have often been the focus of these deceptive narratives, which began proliferating with the surge in violence in early May.

On May 3, when clashes erupted, authorities suspended mobile internet services to prevent the spread of "misinformation and false rumors" on social media platforms. Despite this, misleading content spread rapidly. For instance, a photograph of a woman's corpse wrapped in a plastic sheet went viral on social media. It was falsely identified as a Meitei nurse allegedly raped and killed by Kuki men. This image also circulated widely on WhatsApp groups in Churachandpur district, where clashes began. However, fact-checks revealed that the photo was of Ayushi Chaudhary, a 21-year-old woman murdered in Delhi in November of the previous year.

Similarly, on May 5, another false claim emerged on social media, alleging that the bodies of 37 Meitei women, who had been raped and killed, and the body of a seven-year-old Meitei child, were at the Shija hospital in Manipur's capital Imphal, awaiting post-mortems. This claim was extensively shared in WhatsApp groups across Manipur, with screenshots going viral. However, the hospital clarified that the claims were untrue, stating that as a private medical institution, they were not authorized to conduct postmortems.

Another misleading video surfaced showing the brutal killing of a woman kneeling in the middle of a road while being shot multiple times. The video, falsely attributed to Manipur, was used to depict one community's "violent tendencies." Fact-checks confirmed that the video originated from Myanmar and documented an incident from June 2022, long before the Manipur clashes began. Despite this, the video was shared with hashtags like #Manipur, with some claiming it showed the murder of a Kuki woman. The video's circulation was significant enough for state police to issue warnings against sharing it, emphasizing that legal action would be taken against those who did.

The spread of fake news continued unabated even after the Manipur violence captured national and international headlines on July 19. Some individuals used the crisis to propagate anti-Muslim narratives, aligning with the broader political environment in India that often targets the Muslim community. A notable incident involved a social media claim that a Muslim man was arrested for his alleged involvement in the violence. Tejinder Pal Singh Bagga, a BJP leader, shared this claim on Twitter, garnering millions of views. The claim was misleading, as the police clarified that while a Muslim man had been arrested, the charges were unrelated to the violence against women in Manipur. Even ANI, a prominent news agency, initially reported the arrest inaccurately but later corrected its mistake, attributing the error to a misinterpretation of police communications.

In the tribal-dominated Churachandpur district, a relief camp has been set up near the IB Road District Hospital by the Young Vaiphei Association (YVA) in an old boys' hostel. Zerry, a volunteer at the camp, described how the army and Manipur police conduct regular search operations, often targeting village volunteers—armed locals responsible for community protection. These operations, usually conducted at night or early morning, often result in the confiscation of locally made weapons, which the media portrays as evidence of criminal activity. Zerry explained that most weapons in Kuki-dominated areas are locally crafted due to the lack of funds to purchase sophisticated arms. These weapons are primarily used for self-defense.

Zerry highlighted the double standards in weapon seizures, pointing out that groups in Meitei-dominated areas openly display automatic weapons, including AK-47s and machine guns, on social media without facing similar scrutiny. He alleged that groups like Arambai Tenggol and Meitei Leepun are heavily armed with factory-made weapons and roam freely, yet no significant action is taken against them.

A member of the Indigenous Tribal Leaders' Forum (ITLF) accused the state government of attempting to erase the history and identity of the Kuki-Zo community. She pointed out the stark developmental disparity between the Meitei-dominated valley and the tribal-dominated hills. The valley boasts better colleges, roads, and industries, while areas like Churachandpur remain neglected. Another ITLF member, Ginza Vualzong, lamented that the ongoing conflict has stalled efforts to address the community's longstanding issues.

Zerry also discussed the role of village volunteers, who often hold positions comparable to army personnel in border areas. Armed with single-barrel guns, they ensure the safety of their communities. However, the lack of protection following a 2015 peace agreement between Kuki militant groups and the central government has forced the community to rely on these volunteers for security. Zerry criticized the media for using weapon confiscations to propagate negative narratives about the Kuki community while ignoring the broader context.

Epilogue

As the last words of this book are written, the echoes of Manipur's struggles remain vivid and haunting. The pages you have traversed capture but a sliver of the ongoing narrative of resilience, resistance, and survival. Yet, even as the embers of conflict smolder, the spirit of hope flickers steadfastly.

In the months since the height of the violence, the people of Manipur continue to rebuild their lives piece by piece. The scars of loss are evident, but so too are the seeds of unity sown by those who dare to dream of a peaceful tomorrow. Communities are beginning to bridge divides, and conversations, once silenced by fear, are finding new voices.

This book may conclude here, but the journey toward healing and justice is far from over. Let these stories serve not as a conclusion, but as a reminder of the work that remains. The responsibility lies with all of us—journalists, policymakers, activists, and citizens alike—to remain vigilant, compassionate, and committed to fostering understanding and empathy.

To the people of Manipur, your courage is your legacy. May your voices continue to resonate and inspire. And to the readers, thank you for bearing witness to this chapter of history. May it move you to reflect, to question, and to stand in solidarity with those who fight for justice in the face of adversity.

The flame of Manipur's story burns on, illuminating the path ahead.

www.ingramcontent.com/pod-product-compliance
Lightning Source LLC
LaVergne TN
LVHW090129160826
845673LV00015B/1179

* 9 7 9 8 8 9 6 7 3 6 0 7 3 *